100 FACTS YOU SHOULD KNOW

DINOSAURS

Steve Parker

Gareth Stevens
PUBLISHING

Please visit our website, **www.garethstevens.com**.
For a free color catalog of all our high-quality books, call toll free 1-800-542-2595 or fax 1-877-542-2596.

Cataloging-in-Publication Data

Parker, Steve.
Dinosaurs / by Steve Parker.
p. cm. — (100 facts you should know)
Includes index.
ISBN 978-1-4824-3195-7 (pbk.)
ISBN 978-1-4824-3198-8 (6 pack)
ISBN 978-1-4824-3196-4 (library binding)
1. Dinosaurs — Miscellanea — Juvenile literature.
2. Dinosaurs — Juvenile literature. I. Parker, Steve, 1952-. II. Title.
QE862.P37 2016
567.9—d23

Published in 2016 by
Gareth Stevens Publishing
111 East 14th Street, Suite 349
New York, NY 10003

Copyright © 2016 Miles Kelly Publishing

Publishing Director: Belinda Gallagher
Creative Director: Jo Cowan
Editorial Director: Rosie Neave
Designer: Venita Kidwai
Image Manager: Liberty Newton
Production Manager: Elizabeth Collins
Reprographics: Stephan Davis, Jennifer Cozens, Thom Allaway
Assets: Lorraine King

ACKNOWLEDGMENTS
The publishers would like to thank the following sources for the use of their photographs:
Key: t = top, b = bottom, c = centre, l = left, r = right, m = main. Cover: Roger Harris/Science Photo Library. Alamy: 29 (t) petpics Corbis: 12(t) Louie Psihoyos; 16 Layne Kennedy; 18(cl) Louie Psihoyos; 19 Sciepro/Science Photo Library; 29(b) Walter Myers; 33(t) Handout/Reuters; 42(b) Louie Psihoyos; 43(cr) Louie Psihoyos Glow Images: 35(b) O. Louis Mazzatenta; 44(tl) Lynn Johnson/National Geographic Image Collection; 44(tr) Lynn Johnson/National Geographic Image Collection 45(l) Lynn Johnson/National Geographic Image Collection Science Photo Library: 6–7 Jose Antonio Penas; 18–19 Julius T Csotony; 21 Jose Antonio Penas; 6–27 Christian Jegou Publiphoto Diffusion; 33(b) Christian Darkin; 36–37 Steve Munsinger; 38–39 Christian Jegou; 46(t) Natural History Museum, London Shutterstock.com: 8–9 Eric Broder Van Dyke; 9(t) Catmando; 10(b) leonello calvetti; 12–13 George Burba; 17(b) Catmando; 20 Michael Rosskothen; 21 Marilyn Volan; 22(t) Kostyantyn Ivanyshen; 22(c) Linda Bucklin; 23(bl) DM7; 23(br) Jean-Michel Girard; 30 leonello calvetti; 31(c) Ozja; 31(b) Ralf Juergen Kraft; 47 SmudgeChris The Kobal Collection: 41(b) Moonlighting Films.

All other photographs are from:
Corel, digitalSTOCK, digitalvision, John Foxx, PhotoAlto, PhotoDisc, PhotoEssentials, PhotoPro, Stockbyte.
Every effort has been made to acknowledge the source and copyright holder of each picture. Miles Kelly Publishing apologizes for any unintentional errors or omissions.

Printed in the United States of America
CPSIA compliance information: Batch #CS15GS: For further information contact Gareth Stevens, New York, New York at 1-800-542-2595.

The publishers would like to thank Dinosaur Isle for their help in compiling this book.

DINOSAUR ISLE

DIRECT

DEC - 3 2015

Contents

World of the dinosaurs

1 For more than 160 million years, dinosaurs ruled the land. There were many different kinds – huge and tiny, tall and short, slim and bulky, fast and slow, with fierce sharp-toothed meat-eaters and peacefully munching plant-eaters. Then a great disaster ended their rule.

▼ In South America 70 million years ago, a group of *Austroraptor* dinosaurs attack a huge plant-eater. Many fast, fierce "raptor" dinosaurs had feathers. *Austroraptor* was one of the largest raptors at 600-plus pounds (300-plus kg) and 16 feet (5 m) long.

When were dinosaurs alive?

2 The Age of Dinosaurs lasted from about 230 million to 65 million years ago, during a time called the Mesozoic Era. Dinosaurs were the main creatures on land for 80 times longer than people have been on Earth!

▼ Towards the end of the Paleozoic Era, reptiles replaced amphibians as the main large land animals. Dinosaurs were in turn replaced in the Cenozoic Era by mammals. MYA means million years ago.

3 Dinosaurs were not the only animals living in the Mesozoic Era. There were many other kinds such as insects, spiders, shellfish, fish, scurrying lizards, crocodiles, and furry mammals.

4 There were different shapes and sizes of dinosaurs. Some were small enough to hold in your hand. Others were bigger than a house!

◀ Tiny *Saltopus*, less than 3 feet (1 m) long, was a Triassic close cousin of dinosaurs.

PALEOZOIC ERA

The reptiles, including the ancestors of the dinosaurs, start to become more dominant than the amphibians.

Lystrosaurus (amphibian)

Diplocaulus (mammal-like reptile)

**299–251 MYA
PERMIAN PERIOD**

MESOZOIC ERA

The first true dinosaurs appear. These are small two-legged carnivores (meat-eaters), and larger herbivores, or plant-eaters.

Procompsognathus

Riojasaurus

**251–200 MYA
TRIASSIC PERIOD**

Many different dinosaurs lived at this time, including the giant plant-eaters such as *Barosaurus*.

Barosaurus

Allosaurus

**200–145.5 MYA
JURASSIC PERIOD**

6 There were no people during the Age of Dinosaurs. There was a gap of more than 60 million years between the last dinosaurs and the first humans.

◀ *Stegosaurus* thrived during the late Jurassic Period, in North America and Europe.

5 No single kind of dinosaur survived for all of the Mesozoic Era. Many different types came and went. Some lasted for less than a million years. Other kinds, like *Stegosaurus*, kept going for many millions of years.

MESOZOIC ERA

During the last part of the Age of Dinosaurs, both giant carnivores and armored herbivores were alive.

Tyrannosaurus rex

Deinonychus

Saltasaurus

Spinosaurus

145.5–65.5 MYA
CRETACEOUS PERIOD

CENOZOIC ERA

The dinosaurs have died out, and large mammals soon take over the land.

Megacerops (herbivorous mammal)

65.5–23 MYA
PALEOGENE PERIOD

Newer kinds of mammals become more common, such as cats, horses, whales, and bats.

Thylacosmilus (carnivorous mammal)

Nesodon (therbivorous mammal)

23–2.6 MYA
NEOGENE PERIOD

Before the dinosaurs

7 Dinosaurs were not the first animals on Earth. Many other kinds of creatures lived before them, including different types of reptiles – the group that includes dinosaurs.

▶ *Erythrosuchus* was a crocodile-like reptile that lived before dinosaurs were common.

8 *Dimetrodon* was a fierce, meat-eating reptile. Although it looked like a dinosaur it wasn't one. It lived 270 million years ago, well before the dinosaurs arrived. Dimetrodon was about 10 feet (3 m) long and had a tall flap of skin like a sail on its back.

9 Early crocodiles also looked like dinosaurs. Crocodiles were around even before the first dinosaurs. One was *Erythrosuchus*, which was 15 feet (4.5 m) long, lived 240 million years ago, lurked in swamps and ate fish.

▶ *Dimetrodon's* legs sprawled sideways from its body, like a lizard, rather than being underneath, as in dinosaurs.

10 Therapsids were around before the dinosaurs, and they also lived alongside the early dinosaurs. They were mammal-like reptiles because they didn't have scaly skin like most reptiles. Instead they had furry or hairy skin like mammals.

11 The dinosaur group probably appeared 238–232 million years ago. Lack of fossils means no one is sure when, where, or what were the ancestors. However it is known that the dinosaurs' closest relations include crocodiles and the flying reptiles called pterosaurs, all making up the bigger group termed archosaurs.

▶ *Euparkeria* could probably rear up to run on just its two rear legs – like many meat-eating dinosaurs later.

12 Some small reptiles show what the dinosaurs' ancestors could have looked like. They include *Euparkeria* in South Africa 245 million years ago, and *Lagosuchus* and *Marasuchus* in South America around 235 million years ago. They were small, light and fast, with long back legs, and sharp teeth for feeding on bugs and small creatures.

Dinosaurs arrive

13 The earliest dinosaurs stalked the Earth almost 230 million years ago. They lived in what is now Argentina, in South America. They included *Eoraptor* and *Herrerasaurus*. Both were slim and fast creatures. They could stand almost upright and run on their two rear legs. Few other animals of the time could run upright like this, on legs that were straight below their bodies. Most other animals had legs that stuck out sideways.

ACTUAL SIZE

▲ The teeth of *Eoraptor* were suited to eating both small animal prey and soft plant foods.

The long tail balanced the head and body over the rear legs

Large head with powerful jaws contained saw-edged teeth

▲ *Herrerasaurus* was about 10 feet (3 m) long from nose to tail. It was small, light and fast.

Each foot had three long central toes with sharp claws, and a smaller, shorter toe to each side of these

14 Early dinosaurs hunted small animals such as lizards and other reptiles, insects and worms. They had lightweight bodies and long, strong legs to chase after prey. Their claws were long and sharp for grabbing victims. Their large mouths were filled with pointed teeth to bite and tear up their food.

▶ One of the early big dinosaurs, 2-ton *Lessemasaurus* lived about 210 million years ago in South America.

15 As early dinosaurs spread over the land they began to change, or evolve, into new kinds. Evolution has happened in all living things since life began. New kinds of plants and animals appeared, thrived for a time, and then died out. Some of the early dinosaurs evolved to be much bigger and eat plants, like *Lessemasaurus*, which was 30 feet (9 m) long.

STRONG LEGS!

You will need:
stiff card stock   adhesive tape
safe scissors   paper fastener

1. Copy the picture of Herrerasaurus on page 10 onto card stock, without the rear legs. Color it in on both sides and cut it out.

2. On another piece of card stock, copy the rear legs, color them in, and cut them out.

3. Fix the legs to the body, on either side of the hip area, with the paper fastener. Adjust the angle of the body over the legs. This is how many dinosaurs stood and walked.

First of the giants

16 One of the first big dinosaurs well-known from fossils was *Plateosaurus*. This plant-eater grew up to 26 feet (8 m) long and lived almost 220 million years ago in what is now Europe. It could rear up on its back legs and use its long neck to reach food high in trees.

Long, flexible neck for reaching food high off the ground

Sharp, jabbing claws for defense

Long, strong tail for balance

Powerful back legs for rearing up

▲ Fossils of more than 100 *Plateosaurus* have been found, so its size, shape, teeth, and body details are well known compared to many other dinosaurs.

17 *Riojasaurus* was an even larger plant-eater. It lived 218 million years ago in what is now Argentina. *Riojasaurus* was 33 feet (10 m) long and weighed over one ton – as much as a large family car of today.

18 The first big plant-eating dinosaurs may have become larger, with longer necks, so that they could reach up into trees for food. Their great size would also have helped them fight enemies, since many other big meat-eating reptiles, some as long as 16.5 feet (5 m), were ready to make a meal of them.

◀ Like *Plateosaurus*, *Riojasaurus* was in the dinosaur group called prosauropods, with a small head, long neck, and long tail.

19 These early dinosaurs lived during the first part of the Age of Dinosaurs – the Triassic Period. By its end, 200 million years ago, dozens of kinds of dinosaurs roamed across much of the world.

I DON'T BELIEVE IT!

Early plant-eating dinosaurs did not eat fruits or grasses – there weren't any! They hadn't appeared yet. Instead they ate plants called horsetails, ferns, cycads, and conifer trees.

What teeth tell us

20 We know about dinosaurs and other living things from long ago because of fossils. These are usually hard body parts, such as bones, claws, horns, and scales, that are preserved in rocks for millions of years. Dinosaur teeth were very hard and formed many fossils.

22 The shape of a dinosaur's teeth help to show what it ate. *Edmontosaurus* was a duck-billed dinosaur that was 39 feet (12 m) long. and had rows of broad, wide, sharp-ridged teeth in the sides of its mouth. These were ideal for chewing tough plant foods like twigs and old leaves.

◀ The head of *Edmontosaurus* was long, broad and muscular, suited to spending hours chewing – similar to today's horse.

Toothless beak-like front of mouth

More than 500 chewing back teeth

21 *Tyrannosaurus* had 50–60 long, pointed teeth more than 3 inches (20 cm) long. These were excellent for tearing up victims, and for ripping off lumps of flesh for swallowing. As in other dinosaurs, all through life as old teeth broke or fell out, new ones grew in their place.

▶ *Tyrannosaurus* teeth were strong and stout, but not especially sharp-edged, more suited to tearing than slicing.

14

23 Some dinosaurs, such as *Gallimimus*, had no teeth at all! The mouth was shaped like a bird's beak and made of a tough, strong, horny substance like our fingernails. The beak was suited to pecking up all kinds of foods like seeds, worms and bugs, as many birds do today.

▲ *Gallimimus* was a type of "ostrich dinosaur" with large eyes, a long, lightweight beak and long neck.

24 *Baryonyx* had narrow, pointed, cone-shaped teeth. These resemble the teeth of a crocodile or dolphin today. They were ideal for grabbing slippery prey such as fish.

▲ The head of *Baryonyx* was more than 3 feet (1 m) long, with an expanded, spoon-shaped front snout.

25 The teeth of the giant, long-necked dinosaur *Apatosaurus* were shaped like pencils. They worked like a rake to pull leaves off branches into the mouth, for the dinosaur to swallow.

DINOSAUR TEETH!

With the help of an adult, look in a utensils drawer or toolbox for dinosaur teeth! Some tools resemble the teeth of some dinosaurs, and do similar jobs. File or rasp – broad surface with hard ridges, like the plant-chewing teeth of *Edmontosaurus*. Knife – long and pointed, like the meat-tearing teeth of *Tyrannosaurus rex*. Pliers – Gripping and squeezing, like the beak-shaped mouth of *Gallimimus*.

▲ Although *Apatosaurus* was about 82 feet (25 m) long, its skull measured just 23.6 inches (60 cm). It spent most of its time feeding.

Super-size dinosaurs

26 The true giants of the Age of Dinosaurs were the sauropods. These vast dinosaurs all had a small head, long neck, barrel-shaped body, long tapering tail, and four pillar-like legs. The biggest sauropods included *Brachiosaurus*, *Mamenchisaurus*, *Barosaurus*, *Diplodocus*, *Futalognkosaurus*, and *Argentinosaurus*.

◄ Fossil footprints from a sauropod herd near Purgatoire River, Colorado.

27 Sauropod dinosaurs probably lived in groups or herds. We know this from their footprints, which have been preserved as fossils. Each foot left a print as large as a chair seat. Hundreds of footprints together showed many sauropods walked along with each other.

▲ *Futalognkosaurus*, a type of sauropod known as a titanosaur, was more than 100 feet (30 m) long. Its name, given in 2007, means "giant chief lizard" in the local Argentinian language.

Diplodocus is also known as "Old Whip-tail!" It may have swished its long tail so hard and fast that it made an enormous CRACK like a whip. This living, leathery, scaly whip would scare away enemies or even rip off their skin.

28 **Sauropod dinosaurs swallowed pebbles – on purpose!** Their peg-like teeth could only rake in plant food, not chew it. Pebbles and stones gulped into the stomach helped to grind and crush the food. These pebbles, smooth and polished by the grinding, have been found with the fossil bones of sauropods.

▶ *Brachiosaurus* was about 82 feet (25 m) long and probably weighed in the region of 30 tons. Its amazingly long neck allowed it to browse from the tallest trees.

29 **The biggest sauropods like *Brachiosaurus* and *Futalognkosaurus* were enormous beasts.** They weighed up to ten times more than elephants of today. Yet their fossil footprints showed they could run quite fast – nearly as quickly as you!

30 **Sauropods probably had to eat most of the time, 20 hours out of every 24.** They had enormous bodies that would need great amounts of food, but only small mouths to gather the food.

Killer claws

31 Nearly all dinosaurs had claws on their fingers and toes. These claws were shaped for different jobs in different dinosaurs. They were made from a tough substance called keratin – the same as your fingernails and toenails.

32 *Hypsilophodon* had strong, sturdy claws and was 6.5 feet (2m) long. This small plant-eater probably used them to scrabble and dig in soil for seeds and roots.

33 *Deinonychus* had long, hooked claws on its hands. These helped it to grab victims and tear at their skin and flesh. It also had a huge hooked claw, as big as your hand, on the second toe of each foot. This could flick down like a pointed knife to slash pieces out of prey.

◄ *Deinonychus*, meaning "terrible claw," probably had feathers like other raptors. It lived in North America 110 million years ago.

Long claw on each of the three fingers

Second toe had slashing "terrible claw"

34 *Baryonyx* also had a large claw, but this was on the thumb of each hand. It may have worked as a fish hook to snatch fish from water.

35 *Iguanodon* had claws on its feet. But these were rounded and blunt and looked more like hooves. There were also stubby claws on the fingers, while the thumb claw was longer and shaped like a spike, perhaps for stabbing enemies.

▶ Therizinosaurs, from the Cretaceous Period in Eastern Asia and Western North America, had enormous finger claws; why is a mystery.

36 Giant sauropod dinosaurs had almost flat claws. Dinosaurs such as *Apatosaurus* looked like they had toenails on their huge feet!

▶ The long claw on *Apatosaurus'* front foot was possibly for self-defense.

37 The biggest claws of any dinosaurs, and any animals, belonged to the scythe dinosaurs or therizinosaurs. Their hand claws, up to 3 feet (1 m) long, were perhaps used to pull down and cut off leafy branches as food.

38 Therizinosaurs were big, strange-looking dinosaurs, reaching 33 feet (10 m) long and 5 tons in weight. They lived late in the Age of Dinosaurs, and the group included *Alxasaurus*, *Nothronychus*, *Beipiaosaurus*, and *Therizinosaurus*.

Deadly meat-eaters

Spinosaurus lived about 100 million years ago. It grew to 50 feet (15 m) in length, and weighed as much as 10 tons.

About 42–46 feet (13–14 m) in length, *Carcharodontosaurus* hunted across North Africa 95 million years ago. Its saw-edged teeth were 8 inches (20 cm) long.

Giganotosaurus was up to 44 feet (13.5 m) long and had the largest skull of any meat-eating dinosaur. It lived about 97 million years ago.

39 The biggest meat-eating dinosaurs were the largest predators ever to walk on Earth. *Allosaurus*, which lived 150 million years ago in North America, reached almost 33 feet (10 m) in length, while *Tyrannosaurus rex* from 66 million years ago was 40 feet (12 m). In South America, *Giganotosaurus* was slightly larger, while in North Africa, *Carcharodontosaurus* and *Spinosaurus* were even bigger – the largest meat-eating dinosaurs known so far.

40 These great predators were well equipped for hunting large prey — including other dinosaurs. They had massive mouths with long sharp teeth in powerful jaws. They also had long, strong back legs to run fast, and enormous toe claws for kicking and holding down victims.

41 Meat-eaters probably got food in various ways. They hid behind rocks or trees and rushed out to surprise a victim. Some chased their prey, and others would plod steadily over time to tire out their meal. They might even scavenge — feast on the bodies of creatures that were dead or dying from old age, illness, or injury.

T rex was among the last of the great predatory dinosaurs. It probably weighed 6–7 tons when fully grown.

Allosaurus was the largest meat-eating dinosaur of the Jurassic Period. It was a relative lightweight at only 2–3 tons!

Look! Listen! Sniff!

42 Like the reptiles of today, dinosaurs could see, hear and smell the world around them. We know this from fossils. The preserved fossil skulls had spaces for eyes, ears, and nostrils.

43 Some dinosaurs, such as *Leaellynasaura* and *Troodon*, had big eyes. There are large, bowl-shaped hollows in their fossil skulls to allow for them. Today, animals such as mice, owls and nighttime lizards can see well in the dark. Perhaps *Troodon* prowled through the forest at night, peering in the gloom for small creatures to eat.

▶ *Troodon* was about 6.5 feet (2 m) long and lived in North America 70 million years ago.

▶ *Leaellynasaura*, 10 feet (3 m) long, was a plant-eater from 115 million years ago in what is now Australia.

44 There are also spaces on the sides of the head where *Troodon* had its ears. Dinosaur ears were round and flat, like the ears of other reptiles. *Troodon* could hear the tiny noises of little animals moving about in the dark.

45

The nostrils of *Troodon*, where it breathed in air and smelled scents, were two holes at the front of its snout. With its delicate sense of smell, *Troodon* could sniff out its prey of insects, worms, little reptiles such as lizards, and small shrew-like mammals.

46

Dinosaurs used their eyes, ears, and noses not only to find food, but also to detect enemies — and each other. *Parasaurolophus* had a long, hollow, tube-like crest on its head. Perhaps it blew air along this to make a noise like a trumpet, as an elephant does today with its trunk.

47

Dinosaurs such as *Parasaurolophus* may have made noises to send messages to other members of their group or herd. Different messages could tell the others about finding food or warn them about enemies.

BIG EYES

You will need:

stiff card stock   safe scissors
rubber band   colored pencils

1. Make a *Troodon* mask from card stock. Carefully cut out the shape as shown. Then cut out two small eye holes, each just ½ inch (1 cm) across. Color in your mask.

2. Attach a rubber band so you can wear the mask and find out how little you can see.

3. Make the eye holes as large as the eyes of the real *Troodon*. Now you can have a much bigger, clearer view of the world!

▼ *Parasaurolophus* was a "duck-billed" dinosaur or hadrosaur. It was about 33 feet (10 m) long and lived 80 million years ago in North America.

Living with dinosaurs

48 All dinosaurs walked and ran on land, as far as we know. No dinosaurs could fly in the air or spend their lives swimming in the water. But many other creatures, which lived at the same time as the dinosaurs, could fly or swim. Some were reptiles, like the dinosaurs.

49 Ichthyosaurs were reptiles that lived in the sea. They were shaped like dolphins, long and slim with fins and a tail. They chased after fish to eat.

50 Plesiosaurs were sea-dwelling reptiles. They had long necks, rounded bodies, four large flippers and a short tail.

51 Turtles were another kind of reptile that swam in the oceans long ago. Each had a strong, domed shell, and four flippers. Turtles still survive today. However ichthyosaurs and then plesiosaurs died out by the end of the Age of Dinosaurs.

▶ In this marine and shoreline Cretaceous scene, the dinosaurs *Ouranosaurus* (4) are shown living alongside lots of other types of animals.

52 Pterosaurs were reptiles that could fly. They had thin, skin-like wings held out by long finger bones. Some soared over the sea and grabbed small fish in their sharp-toothed, beak-shaped mouths. Others swooped on small land animals.

53 Birds first appeared about 150 million years ago. Some evolved to dive for fish in the sea, like gulls and terns today. *Ichthyornis* was about 10 inches (25 cm) long and lived along North American coasts.

▲ Unlike modern birds, *Ichthyornis* had tiny teeth in its jaws to grip slippery prey.

Key

1 *Hesperornis* (flightless bird)
2 *Elasmosaurus* (marine reptile)
3 *Pteranodon* (flying reptile)
4 *Ouranosaurus* (dinosaur)
5 *Archelon* (turtle, laying eggs)
6 *Archelon* (turtle, swimming)
7 *Kronosaurus* (marine reptile)
8 *Ichthyosaurus* (marine reptile)
9 Belemnoid (mollusk, similar to modern squid
10 *Mosasaurus* (marine reptile)
11 *Elasmosaurus* (marine reptile)
12 Ammonoid (mollusk)
13 *Cretoxyrhina* (shark)

54 Mosasaurs were huge, fearsome reptiles that appeared later in the Age of Dinosaurs. Related to lizards, they had a massive mouth full of sharp teeth. Some grew to 42 feet (13 m) long and weighed over 5 tons.

How fast?

55 Dinosaurs walked and ran at different speeds, according to their size and shape. In the world today, cheetahs and ostriches are slim with long legs and run very fast. Elephants and hippos are huge heavyweights and plod along more slowly. Dinosaurs were similar. Some were big, heavy and slow. Others were slim, light, and speedy.

▼ *Ornithomimus*, from North America 70–65 million years ago, had long, powerful back legs, and hollow bones (like a bird) to save weight.

56 The fastest dinosaurs were the ostrich dinosaurs, or ornithomimosaurs. They had a similar body shape and proportions to today's biggest and fastest-running bird, the ostrich. *Ornithomimus* was one of the largest, up to 16.5 feet (5 m) long and 660 pounds (300 kg) in weight.

57 *Muttaburrasaurus* was a huge ornithopod type of dinosaur, a cousin of *Iguanodon*. It probably walked about as fast as you, around 2.5 to 3 miles (4 to 5 km) an hour. It might have been able to gallop along at a top speed of 9 miles (15 km) an hour, making the ground shake with its 3-ton weight!

Ankle bones

▶ Fossils of *Muttaburrasaurus* come from Queensland, Australia. This bulky plant-eater had three large toes on each back foot and also three on the smaller front foot.

Foot bones

Toe bones ended in rounded claws

▼ *Coelophysis* was 10 feet (3 m) long. It was one of the earliest dinosaurs, living about 220 million years ago.

58 *Coelophysis* was a slim, lightweight dinosaur. It could probably trot, jump and dart about with great agility. Sometimes it ran upright on its two back legs. Or it could bound along on all fours like a dog at more than 18.5 miles (30 km) an hour.

Built like tanks

59 **Some dinosaurs had body defenses against predators.** These might be large horns and spikes, or thick, hard lumps of bone like armor plating. Most armored dinosaurs were plant-eaters. They had to defend themselves against big meat-eating dinosaurs such as *Tyrannosaurus*.

60 **Triceratops had three horns,** one on its nose and two much longer ones above its eyes. It also had a wide shield-like piece of bone over its neck and shoulders. The horns and neck frill made Triceratops look very fearsome. But most of the time it quietly ate plants. If attacked, Triceratops could charge and jab with its horns, like a rhino today.

▼ *Triceratops* was 29.5 feet (9 m) long and weighed more than 5 tons. It lived 65 million years ago in North America.

Wide neck frill of bone and skin

Long, sharp brow horns

Smaller nose horn

Sharp beak-shaped front of mouth

Wide feet spread great body weight

61 *Styracosaurus* was a ceratopsian ("horn–face") dinosaur, like *Triceratops*, but with a more elaborate neck frill. Up to six horns as long as 3 feet (1 m) extended from the frill's edge, giving this dinosaur an even fiercer appearance.

DESIGN A DINOSAUR!

Make an imaginary dinosaur. It might have the body armor and tail club of *Euoplocephalus*, or the head horns and neck frill of *Triceratops*. You can draw your dinosaur, or make it out of pieces of card or from modeling clay. Give it a made-up name, like *Euoploceratops* or *Tricephalus*. How well protected is your dinosaur? How does it compare to some armored creatures of today, such as tortoises, armadillos, or porcupines?

▲ *Styracosaurus* grew up to 20 feet (6 m) long and was 6 feet (1.8 m) tall at the shoulder.

Tail club made from several fused (joined) bones

Long, straight, powerful tail to swing club

Back covered with bony plates set within the skin

62 *Euoplocephalus* had a great lump of bone on its tail. This measured almost 3 feet (1 m) across and looked like a massive hammer or club. *Euoplocephalus* could swing it at predators to protect itself from attack.

◀ *Euoplocephalus* belonged to the group called ankylosaurs. With big bony sheets and lumps in their skin, they were the most armored of all dinosaurs.

29

Nests and eggs

63 Like most reptiles today, dinosaurs produced young by laying eggs. These hatched into baby dinosaurs that gradually grew into adults.

64 Many kinds of dinosaur eggs and babies have been found. These include those of small, strong-beaked *Oviraptor* from Central Asia and the early sauropod *Massospondylus* from South Africa.

65 Different dinosaurs laid different sizes and shapes of eggs. Huge sauropod dinosaurs such as *Brachiosaurus* probably laid rounded eggs as big as basketballs. Eggs of big meat-eaters like *Tyrannosaurus* were more sausage-shaped, 15.5 inches (40 cm) long and 6 inches (15 cm) wide.

▼ This female *Oviraptor* is checking the newly laid eggs in her nest. Each egg is 5.5–7 inches (14–18 cm) long.

66 Some dinosaurs made nests for their eggs. *Oviraptor* lived more than 75 million years ago in what is now the Gobi Desert of Asia. It probably scraped a bowl-shaped nest in the soil about 3 feet (1 m) across. Into this it laid about 15–20 eggs, in a neat spiral shape.

▲ Studying preserved unhatched eggs (real fossil, left) shows they contained tiny baby dinosaurs (artist's drawing, right).

67 Dinosaur eggs probably hatched after a few weeks or months, depending on how warm it was. The eggshells were slightly leathery and bendy, like most reptile eggshells today, and not brittle or hard like the shells of modern birds' eggs.

▶ Seventy-five million years ago in East Asia, pig-sized *Protoceratops* prepares to defend its nest and eggs from a hungry *Velociraptor*.

68 Fossils of baby dinosaurs show that they looked very much like their parents. However the neck frill of a baby *Protoceratops* was not as large when compared to the rest of its body as in the adult. As the youngster's body grew, the frill grew faster, so its relative size changed. Other dinosaurs' body proportions also changed as they grew bigger.

69 Recent fossil finds show that some dinosaurs looked after their babies, like some reptiles today, such as crocodiles. In one discovery, an adult *Protoceratops* was preserved with some babies just 4–6 inches (10–15 cm) long, probably less than one year old.

Dinosaur babies

70 Some dinosaur parents may have fed their young. Fossils of duckbilled *Maiasaura* include nests, eggs, and newly hatched young. The hatchlings could not move around because their leg bones were not strong enough. Yet their tiny teeth had slight scratches and other marks from eating food. So the parent *Maiasaura* probably brought food, such as leaves and berries, to the nest for them.

▼ In 1978 more than 200 fossils of *Maiasaura* nests, eggs, babies, youngsters and adults were found at a site now known as "Egg Mountain" in Montana. They date to around 75 million years ago.

▲ *Maiasaura* was a plant-eater about 30 feet (9 m) long, belonging to the hadrosaur group. Its newly hatched babies were only 15.7 inches (40 cm) long, but within a year they had grown to 5 feet (1.5 m).

71 The nest of *Maiasaura* was a mud mound about 6.5 feet (2 m) across, with 30–40 eggs and babies. Some fossils show unhatched eggs broken into many small parts, as though squashed by the babies that had already hatched out.

72 Some dinosaurs may even have cared for their young after they left the nest. *Psittacosaurus* was a plant-eater that was 6.5 feet (2 m) long and lived 130–100 million years ago in East Asia. One set of fossils from China suggests that one adult was guarding 34 babies when they all died together, perhaps because the tunnel they were hiding in collapsed.

▼ Fossils of *Psittacosaurus* found in 2003 suggest that one adult may have looked after more than 30 babies.

The end for the dinosaurs

73 About 65 million years ago, the Age of Dinosaurs came to a sudden end. Fossils preserved in the rocks show great changes at this time. However the fossils also show that creatures like fish, insects, birds, and mammals carried on. What happened to kill off some of the biggest, most successful animals the world has ever seen? There are many ideas. It could have been one disaster, or a combination of several.

74 The disaster may have been caused by a giant lump of rock, an asteroid or meteorite. This came from outer space and smashed into the Earth. The impact threw up vast clouds of water, rocks, ash, and dust that blotted out the Sun for many years. Plants could not grow in the gloom, so many plant-eating dinosaurs died. This meant meat-eaters had less food, so they died as well.

75 Many volcanoes around the Earth could have erupted all at the same time, perhaps due to the meteorite impact. They threw out red-hot rocks, ash, dust, and poison gas. Creatures would have choked and died in the gloom.

▼ Scientific studies show that 65.5 million years ago, a space rock smashed into Earth near what is now Yucatán, Mexico.

76 The disaster might have involved a terrible disease. Perhaps this gradually spread among certain kinds of animals and killed them off.

METEORITE SMASH!

You will need:
plastic bowl   flour   large pebble   desk lamp

Put the flour in the bowl. This is Earth's surface. Place the desk lamp so it shines over the top of the bowl. This is the Sun. The pebble is the meteorite from space. Drop the pebble into the bowl. See how the tiny bits of flour float in the air like a mist, making the "Sun" dimmer. A real meteorite smash may have been the beginning of the end for the great dinosaurs.

77 It might be that dinosaur eggs were eaten by a plague of animals. Small, shrew-like mammals were around at the time. They may have eaten the eggs at night as the dinosaurs slept.

What happened next?

78 Other kinds of animals died out with dinosaurs. Flying reptiles called pterosaurs, and swimming reptiles called mosasaurs and plesiosaurs, disappeared. Lots of plants died out too. When a group of living things dies out, it is called an extinction. When many groups disappear at the same time, it's known as a mass extinction.

80 Even though many kinds of animals and plants died out 65 million years ago, other groups lived on. Crabs, shellfish, insects, worms, fish, frogs, and mammals all survived the mass extinction – and these groups are still alive today.

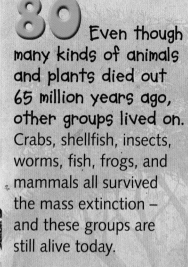

79 Several groups of reptiles also survived the mass extinction. They include crocodiles and alligators, turtles and tortoises, and lizards and snakes. Why some kinds died out in the great disaster, yet other types survived, is one of the main puzzles that experts today are still trying to solve.

Key

1 *Coryphodon* (browsing mammal)
2 *Gastornis* (flightless bird)
3 *Eobasileus* (browsing mammal)
4 *Branisella* (early monkey)
5 *Tremacebus* (early monkey)
6 *Paraceratherium* (browsing mammal)
7 *Arsinoitherium* (browsing mammal)

8 *Hyracotherium* (early horse)
9 *Andrewsarchus* (carnivorous mammal)
10 *Eobasileus* (browsing mammal)
11 *Plesiadapis* (early primate)
12 *Ptilodus* (squirrel–like mammal)
13 *Chriacus* (raccoon–like mammal)

81 After the mass extinction, a different group of animals began to take over the land. These were the mammals. Through the Age of Dinosaurs they were mostly small and skulking, coming out only after dark. Now they could change or evolve to become bigger. Within a few million years they had developed into many kinds, from peaceful plant-eaters to huge, fierce predators.

▼ The mass extinction of 65 million years ago killed big dinosaurs and many other kinds of animals and plants. But plenty of animals survived, especially the mammals.

Myths and mistakes

82 **Some popular ideas about dinosaurs are probably not true.** For example, they are shown in bright colors such as red, yellow, green, and blue. This is guesswork. For dinosaurs and other creatures, there are fossils of skin, and also fossilized feathers, as for *Confuciusornis*. But most, being fossils, have turned to stone, so they do not indicate color. However a few well-preserved feathers show striped patterns, maybe in red and brown.

Toothless beak

Finger claws on wing

83 **For many years, people thought that all dinosaurs were slow and stupid animals.** But we cannot be sure. Some dinosaurs were quick and agile. Also some, like *Troodon*, had big brains for their body size. They may have been quite intelligent.

◀ Head-to-head butting, shown here by *Wannanosaurus*, is no longer thought likely.

84 Another idea was that "bone-headed" dinosaurs (pachycephalosaurs) crashed their heads together. It was thought they did this when fighting for mates or to be leader of the herd, just like rams head-butt today. But their domed skulls would probably slip sideways as they thudded together, causing little damage. Maybe they butted each other in the sides instead.

Wing feathers
(8 inches or 20 cm long)
for agile flight

Wingspan of 27.5
inches (70 cm)

◀ Studies of fossil feathers
from *Confuciusornis*, which
lived 130 million years ago in
China, suggest its plumage
may have been red and black.

85 Another idea grew up that
early cave people had to fight against
dinosaurs and kill them — or the other
way around. But they did not. There was
a very long gap, more than 60 million
years, between dinosaurs such as
Tyrannosaurus and the earliest people.

86 Some people believe that
dinosaurs may survive today in
remote, faraway places on Earth,
such as thick jungle or ocean islands.
But most of the Earth has now been
visited and explored, and no dinosaurs
have been found alive.

Long streamer-like tail feathers
may have been on the male only

▼ In the movie *The Dinosaur Project*
(2012) explorers find living dinosaurs
in Africa's Congo forest. However this
is purely fiction.

I DON'T BELIEVE IT!

One dinosaur's thumb was put on
its nose! When scientists first
dug up fossils of *Iguanodon*,
they found a horn-shaped
bone, which fit
Iguanodon's nose.
Most scientists
now believe that
the spike was a
thumb claw.

How do we know?

▼ Fossils form best in water, such as when drowned dinosaurs were washed by floods into a lake or sea.

1. After death, the dinosaur sinks to the riverbed. Worms, crabs, and other scavengers eat its soft body parts.

2. Sediments cover the hard body parts, such as bones and teeth, which gradually turn into solid rock.

87 We know about long-gone dinosaurs mainly from the fossils of their body parts. These took thousands or millions of years to form, usually on the bottoms of lakes, rivers, or seas, where sand and mud can quickly cover the parts and begin to preserve them. If the animal died on dry land, its parts were more likely to be eaten or rot away.

88 The body parts most likely to fossilize are the hardest ones, which rot away most slowly after death. These include bones, teeth, horns, and claws of dinosaurs and other animals, and also plant parts such as bark, seeds, and cones.

89 Very rarely, a dinosaur or other living thing was buried soon after it died, then a few of the softer body parts also became fossils. These include bits of skin or the remains of the last meal in its stomach.

▲ Bony lumps in the skin of armored dinosaurs such as ankylosaurs fossilize well — the softer skin has rotted away.

3. Huge earth movements move, lift, and tilt the rock layers so they become dry land.

4. Millions of years later the upper rock layers wear away and the fossil remains are exposed.

90
Not all dinosaur fossils are from the actual bodies of dinosaurs. Some are the signs, traces, or remains that they left while alive. These include eggshells, nests, tunnels, footprints, and claw and teeth marks on food.

▲ Dino-dropping fossils come in many shapes and sizes! This scientist is an expert in their study.

91
Dinosaur droppings also formed fossils! They are called coprolites and contain broken bits of food, showing what the dinosaur ate. Some dinosaur droppings are as big as a suitcase!

Digging up dinosaurs

▶ At the excavation site or dig, the first tasks are to make surveys by checking the rock for suitable signs of fossils.

◀ Small bits of rock are scraped away. Workers make notes, draw sketches and take photos to record every stage.

92 **Every year, thousands more dinosaur fossils are discovered.** Most of them are from dinosaurs already known to scientists. But five or ten might be from new kinds of dinosaurs. From the fossils, scientists try to work out what the dinosaur looked like and how it lived, all those millions of years ago.

93 **Most dinosaur fossils are found by hard work.** Fossil experts called paleontologists study the rocks in a region and decide where fossils are most likely to occur. They spend weeks chipping and digging the rock. They look closely at every tiny piece to see if it is part of a fossil. However some dinosaur fossils are found by luck. People out walking in the countryside come across a fossil tooth or bone by chance.

94 Finding all the fossils of a single dinosaur neatly in position is very rare. Usually only a few fossil parts are found from each dinosaur. These are nearly always jumbled up and broken.

▲ After months or years, the restored or "rebuilt" fossil is complete — this is the skull of *Allosaurus*.

◄ Brushes remove bits of dust, soil, and rock flakes. Fragile fossils may be protected with "jackets" of fiberglass or plaster.

95 Dinosaur fossils are studied and rebuilt in paleontology workrooms. They are cleaned and laid out to see which parts are which. It is like trying to put together a jigsaw with most of the pieces missing. Even those that remain are bent and torn. The fossils are put back together, then soft body parts that did not form fossils, such as skin, are added. Scientists use clues from similar animals alive today, such as crocodiles, to help "rebuild" the dinosaur.

QUIZ

1. What do we call a scientist who studies fossils?

2. How is a fossil "dig" recorded?

3. How are fossils packed to protect them?

4. What animals can scientists compare dinosaur fossils with?

Answers:
1. A paleontologist
2. Notes, sketches, and photographs
3. They are put in plaster or fiberglass
4. Crocodiles

43

Dinosaurs today

96 The name "dinosaur" was invented in 1842 by English scientist Richard Owen. He realized that the fossils of some prehistoric creatures were reptiles, but different from any known reptile group. So he made a new group, Dinosauria. Its first three members were *Iguanodon*, *Megalosaurus*, and *Hylaeosaurus*, all from fossils found in England.

▲ Fossil *Sinosauropteryx* has long legs and feet, lower left. Its tail arches up and forwards to its skull, upper right.

▲ The dinosaur *Caudipteryx* from China had tiny arms and fanned-out tail feathers.

97 From the 1850s there was a rush to find hundreds of new dinosaurs in North America. In the 1920s exciting discoveries were made in Central Asia. Today, dinosaur remains are being found all over the world, even in frozen Antarctica. Some of the most amazing fossils in recent years come from Argentina and China.

98 In 1996 fossils of the dinosaur *Sinosauropteryx* showed it had feathers. This slim, fast meat-eater, only 3 feet (1 m) long, lived 123 million years ago in China. Its feathers were thin and thread-like, not designed for flying.

▶ *Microraptor* was one of the smallest raptors ("thief" dinosaurs), just 31.5 inches (80 cm) long.

▲ *Yutyrannus* was one of the biggest feathered dinosaurs, and weighed almost 2 tons. Its fossils are 120 million years old and come from northeast China.

99 Following *Sinosauropteryx*, many more feathered dinosaurs have been found. These include turkey-sized *Caudipteryx*, tiny *Microraptor*, *Dilong*, which is 6.5 feet (2 m) long, and the huge meat-eater *Yutyrannus*, at over 29.5 feet (9 m) in length. But none of these creatures had bodies or feathers designed for flight. However *Archaeopteryx*, which lived 150 million years ago, was a small meat-eater with wide feathers just right for flight.

100 Most experts now believe that birds evolved from small meat-eating dinosaurs. The modern scientific view is that birds are part of the dinosaur group. This means not all dinosaurs died out, or went extinct, 65 million years ago. Some are alive today. They hop, flap, and sing in our gardens, parks, forests, seashores, and other habitats – they are birds.

▶ An early cousin of *Tyrannosaurus*, *Dilong* was also much smaller, about 6.5 feet (2 m) from nose to tail.

I DON'T BELIEVE IT!

The dinosaur with the shortest name was also one of the smallest. *Mei* (meaning "sound asleep") had feathers and was less than 23.5 inches (60 cm) long.

Glossary

conifer: mostly evergreen trees and shrubs having usually needle-shaped or scalelike leaves and including forms with true cones and other fruit

cycad: seed plants that existed especially during the Jurassic and are represented by four surviving families of palmlike tropical plants

dwell: to remain for a time in a certain place

evolution: the process of animals and plants slowly changing into new forms over thousands of years

extinction: the death of all members of a species

herbivore: a plant-eating animal

keratin: a hard substance making up hair, fingernails, horns, and hoofs

meteorite: a space rock that has reached Earth's surface

rasp: a coarse file with cutting points instead of lines

remote: far removed in place or time

scavenge: when an animal eats the remains of dead animals

scrabble: to scratch, claw, or grope about clumsily or frantically

scurry: to move in or as if in a brisk pace

sediment: matter, such as stones and sand, that is carried onto land or into the water by wind, water, or land movement

spiral: a shape or line that curls outward from a center point

For More Information

Books

Brookes, Olivia. *The Rise of the Reptiles*. New York: Windmill Books, 2012.

Gray, Peter. *Everyone Can Draw Dinosaurs*. New York: Windmill Books, 2013.

Shone, Rob. *Oviraptor: The Egg Thief*. New York: PowerKids Press, 2011.

Websites

Believe it or not, birds are actually dinosaurs: Ask a Scientist
http://www.pressconnects.com/story/news/local/2015/02/06/believe-birds-actually-dinosaurs/22936235/
Birds are the last surviving members of the theropods.

New Species Of Long-Necked Dinosaur Discovered In China
http://www.asianscientist.com/2015/02/in-the-lab/species-long-necked-dinosaur-discovered-china/
A dinosaur with a neck more than half its body length found in China.

Palaeontology: The truth about T. rex
http://www.nature.com/news/palaeontology-the-truth-about-t-rex-1.13988
Learn the secrets of the *Tyrannosaurus rex*.

Index